I0450074

Obama
Mania

"Destiny's child"

Yvonne Williams

Outskirts Press, Inc.
Denver, Colorado

The opinions expressed in this manuscript are solely the opinions of the author and do not represent the opinions or thoughts of the publisher. The author has represented and warranted full ownership and/or legal right to publish all the materials in this book.

Obama Mania
Destiny's Child
All Rights Reserved.
Copyright © 2009 Yvonne Williams
V1.0

This book may not be reproduced, transmitted, or stored in whole or in part by any means, including graphic, electronic, or mechanical without the express written consent of the publisher except in the case of brief quotations embodied in critical articles and reviews.

Outskirts Press, Inc.
http://www.outskirtspress.com

ISBN: 978-1-4327-3664-4

Outskirts Press and the "OP" logo are trademarks belonging to Outskirts Press, Inc.

PRINTED IN THE UNITED STATES OF AMERICA

Barack Obama is challenging Americans
to envision a better America.
"O, let America be America again."
—Langston Hughes

Chapter 1
Mystique

Obama mania: Phobia, Prophetic, or just plain Destiny

Who is this rock star Mystique Barack Obama? Is it mania, phobia, prophetic, or just plain destiny?

People are asking who is Barack Obama? Blacks, Whites, Latinos, Native Americans, and Asians are all chanting, "Yes We Can, Yes We Can."

Across the world in China there is a city called Obama, where a group of Chinese women are dressed in traditional Chinese dress, dancing and singing tribute to Obama. "Yes We Can."

In our lifetime are we witnessing the election of the nation's first black president? "Yes We Are."

Who is this man capturing the hearts and minds, the spirit and vision of the 21st century? Well, he's not a rock star, a preacher, or a television celebrity; he's Barack Hussein Obama. A senator, a scholar, the presidential nominee, a man of character, integrity, grace, calm, and charm, and that is something we have not seen in politics in a very long time. Coupled with a personality that radiates geniality and good humor, he is bringing young people, black, white, bipartisan parties together in times of intense economic and foreign challenge. He understands the problems, and sees the potential for change that must be delivered.

"There is no such thing as inevitable war. If war comes it will be from failure of human wisdom." —Bonar Law

And I might add that wisdom must be demonstrated by the American president, by a show of patience, restraint, compassion, strength, and courage in the struggle for solutions.

Barack Obama, like Benjamin Banneker, is "fresh proof that the powers of the mind are disconnected with the color of the skin." —James McHenry, Secretary of War under President John Adams

Some people make jokes about his name; they can't get past the man running for president with the funny name. They say they won't vote for a man with a name like Obama. How stupid is that? It seems prejudiced not to vote for someone because you don't like the sound of his last name.

A research of his full name "Barack Hussein Obama" means good, honest, and blessed one. Barack, spelled Barak, is first found in the book of Genesis 1:22, and found 320 more times in the Bible. And my final comment about funny names—here are a couple that I found funny at first and hard to pronounce: Schwarzenegger and Kweisi Mfume. So to all the people who have prejudices about funny, odd, and unusual names, get over it and move on. **We have a country to save!**

Barack Obama is a man who has generated new leadership, a man with a clear vision, a reformer, a man who can grasp the complex dynamics of our country and imagine a future grounded in the best for all people.

Cornel West in *Race Matters*: "Freedom, democracy, and equality must be invoked to invigorate all of us. Especially those who have lost the audacity to hope. Only visionary leadership can motivate 'the better angels of our nature' as Lincoln said, and to activate that leadership deserves cultivation and support. This new leadership is grounded in grassroots organizing that highlights democratic accountability in the 21st century. This challenge will be to help Americans determine whether a genuine multicultural democracy can be created and sustained in an era of global economy and moment of mania."

"Let us dare to hope and pray that the intelligence, imagination, wit, and courage of Americans will not fail us. Either we learn a new language of empathy and compassion, or this time the fire will consume us all." —Richard Wright, *12 Million Black Voices 1941*.

Chapter 2
Candid Crucial

"The differences between black folk and white folk are not blood or color, and the ties that bind us are deeper than those that separate us. The common road of hope which we all traveled has brought us into a stronger kinship than any words, laws, or legal claims. The proper starting point for a candid crucial debate about race in America is now! When racial stereotypes question the fact that a black man does not have experience, what they are saying is that he does not have the intellectual talent to be running for the highest office in the land, nor is he entitled to the office of the President of the United States of America." —Cornel West, *Race*

Matters.

Barack Obama is the symbol of America's possibilities; some say he is elitist and arrogant, and when he acts presidential they say he is presumptuous. I believe Americans prefer confidence instead of false modesty, change instead of same. But a new America is speaking out, a progressive America, a We-Want-Change America. Don't be fooled. The so-called GOP (Good Old Party) is not the good old party; it's more of the same McCain, Palin, Bush.

Chapter 3
The Bloggers:
Join the Disscusion

There is nothing good about recession, depression, deception, banks closing, soaring gas prices, lay-offs.

Yes, I'm clinging to my Bible.

Do you think America is ready for a black president?

YES, YES, and YES.

NO, NO, NO.

I'm going hunting.

What happened to his plane? Oops! Another plane please.

Let's do away with divisive bi-partisanship.

<u>Obama:</u>

"We can't afford to be divided by race, we can't afford to be divided by region or by class, we can't afford to be divided by gender. We are one family, one people, one America."

The Bloggers: Join the Discussion

Let's do away with old rhetoric, old politics, and old of the same.

Karl Rove needs to be held accountable. Go to contempt for Karl Rove.com

Corruption in the Justice Dept

Greetings from Australia, I have been watching all of the interviews, especially Gov. Sarah Palin's, I can't believe this is the best Americans have to offer.

Change you can count on

Change we can deliver
Yes We Can!

We Get It!

Barack Gets It!

We need reform

Bush/McCain/Palin – There are few statesmen to-day who so definitely and clearly measure up to an affirmative answer to these four questions: History will ask, "Did the man have integrity? Did the man have courage? Did the man have unselfishness? Did the man have consistency?" You decide.

Obama/Biden – Both hold constitutional law de-grees, educated and cool, and definitely affirmative to measuring up to all four questions.

Bush/McCain/Palin are not what this country needs.

Dumb and Dumber – Whoa!

Women for Obama

Seniors for Obama

Youth for Obama

Students for Obama

Americans for Obama

Next Generation Veterans for Obama
Military Families for Obama

Gov. Sarah Palin, you shouldn't knock community organizers. Remember that Jesus who saved you was a community organizer and Pontius Pilate was a governor.

Republicans for Obama. Yes, Colin Powell praised Obama with "I think he's been an exciting person on the political stage. He has energized a lot of people in America. He has energized a lot of people around the world... I think he is worth listening to."

Republican Congressman Jim Leach endorsed Barack Obama for president, saying Obama's platform is one of "old American values that are as much a part of the Republican as the Democratic tradition."

Chapter 4
The Bank Heist

Recession: Economics-Meltdown October 2008
WAR ON AMERICA

It is the worst financial meltdown since the Great
Depression.

They have bankrupt America. There is no money in
the treasury; they spent our money on the Iraq war
and bailing out failing banks. There is no money for
the next president.

The Biggest Bank Heist in American History

Indy Mac bank just went bust; mortgage giants Fannie Mae and Freddie Mac are in trouble; Lehman Brothers is in trouble; AIG is in trouble, and 100 more banks are predicted to have major problems.

How is this for SHOCK and AWE. They want the American people to fund the WAR ON AMERICA. They have bankrupted America and want to bill the American people for the privilege. This is insane.

There is no money for the next president! Americans are the losers in all of this. No bailout for us!?

You can forget about grants or asking for money to save the whales, dolphins, or any other endangered species. For the last eight years, they have robbed the treasury, and there is no money to bail out the homeowners facing home foreclosures.

Jesus warned about the money changers.

John McCain is part of the foxes in the henhouse with no oversight! He supported de-regulation of the banking industry, and he was one of the Keating Five S & L bank scandal. Read about it!

John McCain said the economy was fundamentally strong. **How wrong** he was; his camp sent him back out 24 hours later to retract his statement.

Breaking News! Republicans Revolt against

Bush/McCain Bailout Plan

Stocks plunged after the failure of a 700-million-dollar bailout plan. John McCain asked his Republican camp to vote for the bailout plan, but his party's NO VOTE by the House was a rejection, a revolt against the Bush/McCain party. It's simple. John McCain didn't deliver the votes. This was John McCain's 3 a.m. call. And he did not pass the test!

Chapter 5
The 1929 Great Depression Remembered

"All Fall Down" by Winnie Lee Smiley

"Nature knew the destructive fall that was destined to occur."

The depression minus many, 1929, an entire nation self-destructed, the stock market crashed, banks closed their doors, and instantly people lost everything they owned. The rich became poor, the poor became poorer.

The 1929 stock market crash had actually begun to take hold weeks before the final impact. There had been numerous dispelled speculations and related articles in the newspapers for several months prior to the end of October, but most had been dismissed as just "rumors and fallacy." Hadn't Hoover pulled the Russians out of their near starvation, and hadn't he also hastily come to the aid of the State of Mississippi during the devastating floods? Surely with the overwhelming majority vote President Hoover had received, the people couldn't possibly have been wrong in their judgment. The consensus was that with Herbert Clark Hoover in the White House, things would be back to normal in no time – but the fateful day reached its climax when prime stocks of major corporations nationwide fell on an average of near 40 points in a single day, and an estimated 16,000,000 shares were dumped on the New York Stock Exchange.

October 24, 1929 would be known throughout history as "Black Thursday"; yet, Tuesday, October 29, 1929 would be the day most remembered. In less than three weeks' time a devastating multibillion-dollar loss incurred on the stock markets. Mass panic and unprecedented poverty were the instant results of the great disaster.

Millions of lives ended or were drastically changed with the financial crash. As a result, the entire country was thrown into the throes of the most disastrous depression in its history.

The greater population was suddenly forced to subsist on a near starvation diet. Thousands were reduced to standing in line for hours in freezing and sweltering hot weather in what quickly came to be known as the "soup lines."

The headlines screamed the plight of the nation. Crowds wrestled and fought to gain admittance to banks whose doors had closed forever – locking out dreams of a lifetime. Large and small businesses ceased all operations without notice. Where sunken ocean liners and gangland killings had formerly led the top news of the day – they were replaced with stories of law-abiding, angry citizens now struggling to survive and questioning how did this happen? The disastrous revelations of the times were shouted on every street corner,

EXTRA! EXTRA! READ ALL ABOUT IT!

BANK ROBBERIES! BUSINESSES COLLASPSE!

MORTGAGE FORECLOSURES!

EXTRA! EXTRA! READ ALL ABOUT IT!

For the rich and powerful who had been forewarned – many of whom relied on Swiss banks to keep their fortunes intact – nothing changed. The languid cruises to the Riviera, long nights in casinos, and croquet games in the late afternoons on vast, rolling lawns remained exactly the same, untouched by poverty. They traveled to foreign mountainous countries for gala ski trips. They boarded luxury liners and sailed to the islands until they tired. Once bored with that, they traveled home to throw lavish parties for their friends.

Ironically, only minutes away, hungry children and grownups alike huddled together, homeless, lining the streets, alleys, parks, and highways – begging – always begging for a bite to eat. Some had been bankers, businessmen, and investors; others were planters and small farmers who had owned multiple acres of land passed down for generations –lost to them overnight. They were white- and blue-collar workers and just plain ex-workers.

President Hoover remained optimistic, and articles under foreboding headlines quoted him:

"We will come out of this into a period of prosperity greater than ever before. We shall do so this time."

Yet, the depression did not end as predicted. Conditions rapidly worsened. Millions were terminated and remained jobless. October 29, 1929 was only the genesis of the great depression. Yet to come was the ill-fated, mind-plunging aftermath.

Chapter 6
Wake up America

Lest we forget!

Wake up, America! Listen up! Wake up, America!
Look around, it's October 2008 and today we are
facing a financial crisis! America has to do a new
thing. We have a new generation of Americans who
are ready for change! This new generation is em-
powered to do hard things; this new generation is
energized and ready to deliver. A Rebirthing of
America! An Economic Cleansing, Reform, Barack
Obama for Change!

"I am for any movement whenever there is a good

cause to promote, a right to assert, a chain to be broken, a burden to be removed, or a wrong to be redressed." —Frederick Douglass

<u>Stimulus Checks:</u>

I never saw my stimulus check; the IRS took my $1,200 stimulus check and put it toward my 2004 back tax of $1,168 dollars. I received a whopping 42 dollars. What president was it who said the American people can use that stimulus check to spend it any way and on whatever they want to boost the economy? Uhmmmmm. **They just forgot to tell the American people, Oh, by the way, if you owe back taxes, your stimulus check will be used to pay that back tax.**

Bloggers: join the discussion

Obama **voted for** veteran's benefits; McCain voted **against** them. Who really supports the military?

Expect to see more Republicans jump ship closer to the election. It's difficult to walk away from your nominee, but you have to put your country first.

The only Democrat for McCain is Joe Lieberman, as he is practically a Republican by now.

It's kind of nice to hear about Obama Republicans after all the years we have had to hear about the so-called Reagan Democrats. NICE…

Sean Hannity on Extramarital Affairs. John Edwards and John McCain, uhmm... Did you say that any presidential nominee who had an extramarital affair is not fit to be president? Sean, who will you vote for?

Homeowners facing foreclosure, renegotiate the principle because the Feds spent your money. Oops sorry! No more money in the treasury! Can't bail you out! We have some trailers left over from Katrina!

Is there no bailout for US?

If we have the ability to set minimum wages, we should have the ability to set maximum wages.

Chapter 7
Listen to the Children

Remembrance by Rebecca M. Wolfold

The Statue of Liberty stands shaking her fist in anger and pain

But she remembers how much patriotism we will gain

Firefighters go out risking their lives to save others

While other people sit home wishing they had their sisters or brothers

21

Some people were there, watching the towers fall from the sky

Some watched on television, people suffer and die

They thought we would fear them and be divided

After all that has happened, we still stand here united.

** Listen up, America, the truth is, Iraq wasn't responsible for this inferno, Bush/McCain had it wrong. They went after the wrong enemy. Barack Obama had it right. He opposed this war from the beginning because he knew it was the wrong enemy. Unpack your backpack to Iraq.

Polar Bear by Hannah Bennett

Polar Bear, oh Polar Bear

Because some people do not care, soon you will be very rare

Polar Bear, Polar Bear

If they destroy your snowy home, then you'll have no place to roam

Polar Bear, Oh, Polar Bear

You have been hunted from year to year
I hope that you will never disappear

Polar Bear, Oh, Polar Bear

I'll try to help you if I fear that you will not be here next year.

** Governor Sarah Palin, are you listening? God loves the moose and caribou too.

America Last:

Hurricane Katrina – America Last? The United States is sending billions of dollars in aid to the country of Georgia. What about our own men and women, 5,000 of whom are still living in trailers three years after Katrina hit? Uhmmmmm.

The Prophet at Harvard, nooooo, not Barack, ha, ha. Dinesh D'Souza reports on Alexander Solzhenitsyn, uhmmm another funny name, and highlights Solzhenitsyn's 1978 address whether to indicate the West such as it is today is a model country; his answer was negative. The press, he says, has become the greatest power within the Western countries, more powerful than legislature, the executive, and judiciary. One would then like to ask: by what law has it been elected and to whom is it responsible?

Hear this, Sean Hannity: Solzhenitsyn goes on to say how many nasty, immature, superficial, and misleading judgments are expressed every day, confusing readers, and without any verification. A shameful intrusion into the privacy of people under false slogans: everyone has the right to know everything. The whole address is worth reading, even if you don't agree with everything.

Just for the record, Larry Elder, Sean Hannity, and Bill O'Reilly: I listen to your radio shows for one reason, because scripture tells us to keep our enemies close. Time after time, I've listened to you and your callers bash Democrats on these issues, as if Republicans hold the monopoly on Christianity. Well, I am a proud Democrat, I am a proud United States Army Veteran, I proudly fly the American flag outside my home, I am a Christian who believes that Jesus Christ is Lord and Savior of my life, and I believe that human life starts at conception.

Chapter 8
Echo

Barack Obama is a wise man. "A wise man thinks before he speaks." —KJV

"The test of what makes a leader is not who shouts the loudest or gets the angriest but who gets the most results." —Whitney Moore Young

I decided to write this book because I wanted to "lift my voice and sing." I wanted to lend voice to and echo the same "Dreams of our Forefathers," the prophetic speeches of great men and women, of Martin Luther King, Jr.'s "I Have A Dream," Sojourner Truth's "Ain't I a Woman," Frederick

Douglass, Booker T. Washington, John F. Kennedy, speeches and songs that changed the character of America and its people. "O, let America be America again," by Langston Hughes. "Character, Not Circumstances, Makes the Man," Booker T. Washington.

American me! They have taken jobs from American me, they have taken money from American me, they have taken America from American me, poem excerpts by Michael Anthony Adams. Tavis Smiley TV host and commentator, from his book *Doing What's Right*. "Do not abandon the climb, when you succeed, more likely than not it will be against the odds."

Chapter 9
My Voice

There is change happening, and I am a small part of this larger plan. Let me explain the event of the time when I came to the realization that I, too, needed to "lift my voice and sing." It was the year 2000. I was a nurse working in the operating room when the doctor I was working with went on a verbal racist tirade against me. He verbally and racially harassed me for over an hour, while he was operating on his patient! He hurled one racial insult after another, stopping during the operation to look up at me and say, "I would hate to be born a black man in America. You people have it hard. I would never let my daughter marry a black man, and she knows better."

He said he didn't think it was right for people to mix. "The race should be pure. A pure white race, that's how it should be, not zebras!" He said that you don't see monkeys and horses mixing, or other animals mixing. A pure white race, he said, that's how it should be. He said where he came from there were no black people and that he was white and just didn't think we should mix. He also went on to say, "You blacks are separating yourselves by having your own black colleges for blacks only, your own black magazines, and your own black TV stations." He said that if he had to be born black, he'd want to be Michael Jordan or Michael Jackson because they have lots of money. He said that you don't see No Colored Allowed signs posted on doors anymore, and that he hated all this politically correct crap, and people are afraid to tell the truth. He said black people need to score 1400, or a perfect 1600, on the SATs to get accepted to Harvard or Stanford. He said, "What do you think? They're just going to let you people get in without working hard? You blacks have to work harder and you'll get in." He said that black doctors are working in ghetto areas of Los Angeles because they can't compete at the good hospitals. He also said that country music is good music, pure white music, and blacks don't like country music.

He said this and much more that day in the operating room while operating on his patient. It took everything I had within me to remain professional, not chew him out, give him a history lesson about blacks in America, why we have historically black colleges, black entertainment TV, magazines, etc. Now, I can appreciate and engage in a sincere, honest dialogue on race in America, but that wasn't his intent. His intent was to racially harass, demean, insult, and humiliate me. I remained quiet and professional out of respect for myself, my nursing profession, and the oath "aeger primo," meaning "patient first." I felt betrayed and disdain for this doctor's display of unprofessional behavior. But I found strength knowing that most doctors that I work with are not like him, and I remembered the words of James Weldon's song and thoughts "that I will not allow one prejudiced person or one million or one hundred million to blight my life. I will not let prejudice or its attendant humiliations and injustices bear me down to spiritual defeat. My inner life is mine, and I shall defend and maintain its integrity against all the powers of hell."

Chapter 10
Ferris Bueller's Day Off – Sound Familiar?

John McCain suspended his campaign for a day. John McCain telephoned David Letterman to cancel his appearance on the show, saying that he "had to rush back to Washington to work on the Wall Street bailout plan, for the economy was cratering." But TV monitors caught John across town interviewing with Katie Couric, same time, same night! Whoops! David Letterman did not take too kindly to being lied to. A Maverick – NOT! – John McCain is no maverick; John McCain is a gambler, and we will not let him gamble away the future of America. Why should we pay for mistakes made by McCain and his friends? Mistake number one. His selection of Gov. Sarah Palin was hasty, reckless, and showed poor judgment. Listen to her interview. Mistake number two. He told the American people that the economy was "fundamentally strong." Not true. The next day it went BUST! Mistake three. McCain suspended his campaign. Senator Obama said, "A president has to be able to multi-task, if need to, fly to Washington, take care of business, then hop on another plane to fly to Mississippi for a debate." Did McCain need a siesta? A nap? A rest? Or did he need to re-group because his numbers in the polls were dropping?

Why should we pay for mistakes made by John McCain and his friends? We will not give him four more years to gamble away the White House.

Gov. Sarah Palin of Alaska is feisty, energetic, witty, and she seems nice enough; however, nice enough is not good enough! The stakes are much higher here. This is not a high school prom queen challenge or a beauty pageant. Unfortunately, she shares the same message, more of the same divisive, non-unifying, non-substantive, warmongering, attack dog republican rhetoric. We cannot have a governor learning on the job! During a recent television interview, Gov. Palin was asked about her foreign policy experience. Her answer was "I can see Russia from my house. And Putin flies over my house when he comes from Russia." What? I was totally confused by her answer – complete gibberish, gobbledygook. During another interview, Palin was asked by Katie Couric three times to give specific examples of John McCain's position on pushing for more regulations in the past 26 years, and she responded, saying, "I will go find some examples and bring 'em back to ya!" What? Is this really the best the republicans can do for VP pick? This is the second highest office in America. **WE'RE IN TROUBLE.** Guys and gals, it's simple. The first Dude Todd Palin and the Gov. Sarah are not ready for Washington, and we cannot have a governor learning on the job!

Recently First Dude Todd Palin flat out refused to respond when subpoenaed to testify about his role in the Trooper gate scandal and possible abuse of legislative powers by him and his wife Governor Sarah Palin. They aren't even in the White House and are already showing signs of covering up scandals. My goodness, when does it end, the lies, the hypocrisy, the cover-ups, the bailouts for the rich, while the homeowners struggle to stay in their homes, facing mortgages, foreclosures; where's the relief for the people? Bail the people out. Rescue the people. I am sick and tired of this Republican Bush/McCain administration using fear tactics to scare the Americans to get what they want. I can't wait for real change. Remember Katrina, the convention center, where people were left without food or water in one big smelly septic tank in New Orleans? Children were raped, and people died, and this administration did nothing! It's unconscionable, inhumane and outrageous! Wake up, people! This administration doesn't give a hoot about you.

Governor Palin wanted library books destroyed at a local library in Alaska, but the librarian stood her ground and basically told Gov. Palin: You will **not** remove or destroy these books.

ENOUGH IS ENOUGH!

We will not tolerate any more cover-ups! The American people will not be fooled any longer! And we will not give you four more years to give us HELL on Earth!

The SURGE in Iraq – I'm tired of hearing that the surge in Iraq is working. The question was never about the surge working. The goal was to get the Iraqis to take control of their country. Obama had it right from the beginning; he opposed this war from the beginning. He got it then and still gets it.

Barack Obama gets it and the millions of Americans who voted for him get it; young people get it, and people from around the world get it. This is why we need change, change that we can count on! Obama.

Barack Obama is challenging Americans to envision a **better** America! The DNC convention in Denver was a down payment on that dream, the promissory note of "Life, Liberty, and the Pursuit of Happiness." The torch is being passed to a new generation of Americans – committed to hope and confidence for the future.

Do not abandon the climb.

Acknowledgments

To those who have inspired and encouraged me,

My family, the Williams, Woodfords and Smileys

My children – George, aka the Original Youngbuck, Victoria, Andre Jr., Terrell, Shawn, and Megan

My grandchildren, Jahbez and Judah and a third on the way

My pastor, Michael Mancha

Associate Pastor, Charlie Briggs

Sharon Mancha, Ministries.com. Your book, *The Power of Intimacy with Christ,* inspired me the more

My Eagle Vision Community Church family

My very special cousin Winnie "Franny" Dotson

Tuskegee University Army ROTC

Tuskegee Airmen Flight Medical Doctor, Hackley E. Woodford, MD

Kappa Alpha Psi Fraternity

Dedication

This book is dedicated to my father-in-law, Doctor Homer L. Williams, MD, who I wish could have been here to witness this historical time in history.

To the darker brother whose tomorrow has come

To my brown and red brothers, you, too, are America

To my white brother, remember King's "Dream"

www.ingramcontent.com/pod-product-compliance
Lightning Source LLC
Chambersburg PA
CBHW061227280526
45784CB00006B/2671